TECHNOLOGY
MYSTERIES REVEALED

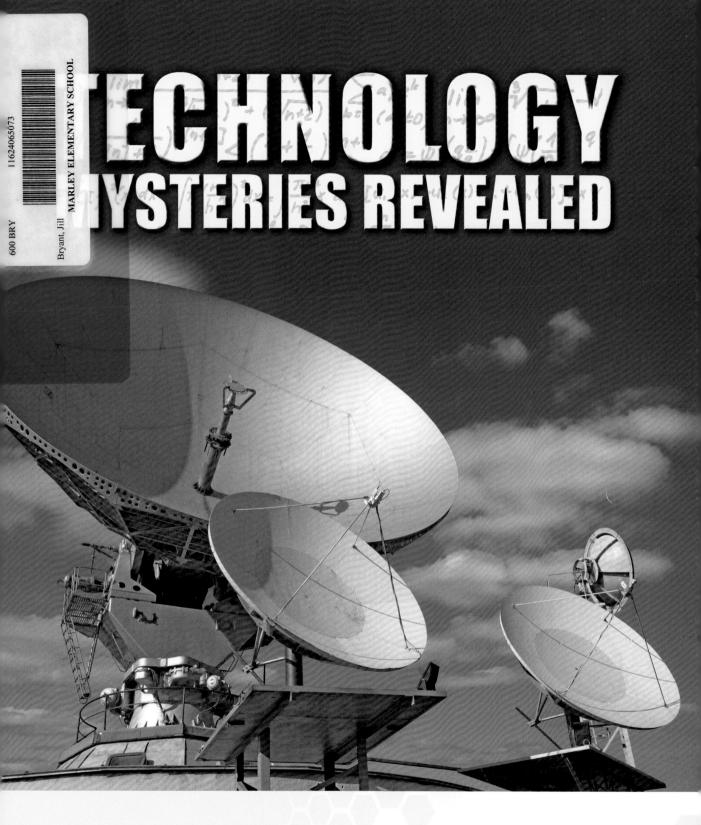

Jill Bryant

Author: Jill Bryant

Editor: Molly Aloian

Proofreader: Crystal Sikkens

Project coordinator: Kathy Middleton

Production coordinator: Katherine Berti

Prepress technician: Katherine Berti

Project editor: Tom Jackson

Designer: Paul Myerscough,
Calcium Creative

Picture researcher: Clare Newman

Managing editor: Tim Harris

Art director: Jeni Child

Design manager: David Poole

Editorial director: Lindsey Lowe

Children's publisher: Anne O'Daly

Photographs:
Alamy: Dburke: p. 16; Jeff Morgan, Alternative Technology:
p. 29 (top)
Corbis: Richard Cohen: front cover
Istockphoto: David P. Lewis: p. 10 (bottom)
JI Unlimited: p. 9 (bottom), 19 (top), 22 (top), 27 (bottom)
NASA: MSFC: p. 14, 28
Photolibrary: Henry Beeker/Age Fotostock: p. 15 (top)
Science & Society Picture Library: Science Museum: p. 20
Science Photo Library: Sam Odgen: p. 23
Shutterstock: Aslani13.com: p. 30; Thomas Barraf: p. 25;
Joe Gough: p. 21 (top); Jason Grower: p. 13 (top);
Michael Heiber: p. 29 (bottom); Melissa King: p. 21
(bottom); Holly Kuchera: p. 8–9; Peter Kylio: p. 22
(bottom); Tobias Machhaus: p. 7; Peter Macs: p. 11;
Monkey Business Media: p. 8 (bottom); Wessel Du Plooy:
p. 17 (bottom); Vadim Ponomarenko: p. 1; Olesia Ru &
Ivan Ru: p. 27 (top); Thomas Sztanek: p. 4–5; Graham
Taylor: p. 17 (top); Virgin Galactic: p. 13 (bottom);
Zoommer: p. 26; ZTS: p. 10 (top)

Illustrations:
Geoff Ward: p. 15 (bottom)

Series created by Brown Reference Group

Brown Reference Group have made every attempt to
contact the copyright holders of all pictures used in this
work. Please contact info@brownreference.com if you
have any information identifying copyright ownership.

Library and Archives Canada Cataloguing in Publication

Bryant, Jill
    Technology mysteries revealed / Jill Bryant.

(Mysteries revealed)
Includes index.
ISBN 978-0-7787-7417-4 (bound).--ISBN 978-0-7787-7432-7 (pbk.)

    1. Technology--Juvenile literature. I. Title.
II. Series: Mysteries revealed (St. Catharines, Ont.)

T48.B79 2010   j600   C2009-906257-7

Library of Congress Cataloging-in-Publication Data

Bryant, Jill.
    Technology mysteries revealed / Jill Bryant.
        p. cm. -- (Mysteries revealed)
    Includes index.
    ISBN 978-0-7787-7432-7 (pbk. : alk. paper)
    -- ISBN 978-0-7787-7417-4 (reinforced library binding : alk. paper)
    1. Technology--Juvenile literature. I. Title. II. Series.

T48.B8578 2010
600--dc22

2009042772

Crabtree Publishing Company

www.crabtreebooks.com   1-800-387-7650

Printed in the U.S.A./122009/BG20091103

Published in Canada
Crabtree Publishing
616 Welland Ave.
St. Catharines, Ontario
L2M 5V6

Published in the United States
Crabtree Publishing
PMB 59051
350 Fifth Avenue, 59th Floor
New York, New York 10118

Contents

Introduction

Scientists solve mysteries and make discoveries— and to do that they need to ask questions. Once they have figured out how stuff works, they can use it to make better technology.

Scientists are a bit like detectives. They look at the facts and then tell us what they all mean. To a scientist, a fact is something that can be measured, such as the weight of a metal or the speed of the wind. Scientists collect facts by observing things carefully. Often, it is a mystery why things happen the way they do. Scientists come up with a theory that might explain the mystery. They then do **experiments**, or tests, to check whether their idea is true.

Being useful

Okay, so scientists are slowly solving mysteries, so we know more and more about how the Universe and everything in it works. Why is that important? To answer that question you need to meet an engineer. Engineers are a bit like scientists—they use math a lot and measure things very carefully. However, engineers are not trying to come up with new theories about the Universe. Instead, they are using scientific knowledge to make new machines and other pieces of technology.

Inside inventions

This book looks at different areas of technology. Engineers have invented many of the technologies covered in this book, but many are still a mystery to people. How does it all work?

technology The name for all the useful tools and machines people have invented

⬤ Engineers use their
knowledge of science
to make machines
work better.

How do you make electricity from sunlight?

There are two ways: You can trap the energy in light or use the heat coming from the Sun to power a generator.

Photovoltaic cells—or solar cells—make small amounts of electricity when sunlight shines on them. When light strikes the photovoltaic cell, **electrons** are knocked off the material in the cell. The electrons flood into wires running through the solar cells, forming a current of electricity. Photovoltaic cells are grouped together, forming a large panel.

Heat not light

In places where the Sun's rays are very hot, electricity is made using solar thermal power plants. They have hundreds of curved mirrors, which concentrate the sunlight onto pipes full of liquid. The liquid may be water or perhaps alcohol, which boils even more easily. The heat from the sunlight boils the liquid into a gas, or vapor. The vapor spreads out and pushes along the pipes until it reaches a **turbine**. The gas spins the turbine and drives an electricity generator.

> "The two most common forms of power on Earth are sunlight and wind, and they're getting cheaper and cheaper."
>
> Ed Begley, Jr.

electrons Tiny particles inside all substances; electricity is a flow of electrons

Solar panels ▷
work well during
the day, but what
happens if you
need electricity
at night?

AMAZING!

The first solar power
experiments took place in the
1860s when French inventor
Auguste Mouchout tested the
first solar-powered motor. Like
many people today, Mouchout
believed we should use
less coal and other
polluting fuels.

turbine A high-tech windmill that spins around in wind or water

Why does a rubber band always spring back after being stretched?

Rubber is a curious material called a **polymer**. In other words, the rubber is made up of billions of tiny strings, way too small to see. Inside the rubber band, the strings are wildly tangled up. When you pull on a rubber band, however, something strange happens. The tangled strings stretch out nice and straight so the rubber stretches into a longer shape. When you let go, the strings get all messed up again, which makes the rubber band bounce back to its smaller shape. Stretching like this is called being elastic.

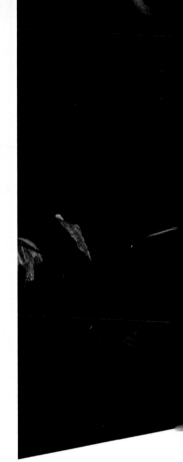

◀ Rubber bands were invented 150 years ago.

polymer A type of chemical made up of long chains of smaller chemicals

How do you make an alloy?

To make an alloy, you mix up metals. When metals are heated to a high temperature they melt into liquids. As you pour one liquid metal into another, both types of **atoms** will mix together. The mixture then cools and hardens into an alloy. Alloys are usually stronger and harder than pure metals. Some common alloys are bronze, brass, and steel. Bronze is copper mixed with tin. Brass is made from copper and zinc. Steel contains iron and carbon mixed with several other metals.

⬤ Hot metals mix together like salt mixing into warm water.

HISTORY EXPLAINED

The Bronze Age is a time in history when the alloy bronze was the most high-tech material anyone could make. Knives, weapons, tools, and jewelry were made from bronze. The Bronze Age occurred after the Stone Age and before the Iron Age. Bronze was more useful than stone, but not as strong as iron. Because bronze was discovered at different times around the world, different people had their Bronze Ages at different times. In the world's most ancient places—Mesopotamia, India, and China—the Bronze Age began about 5,500 years ago. In Europe, it was about 3,900 years ago. Native Americans did not begin working with copper and other metals until 1,300 years ago.

⬤ This bronze pot was made thousands of years ago in what is now Jordan.

atom The smallest unit of a substance; there are 90 types of atoms, including all metals

What have nonstick pans and outdoor clothing got in common?

Both use a weird and wonderful solid called polytetrafluoroethylene, or Teflon for short. It was discovered by accident in the 1930s. It is a super slippery plastic that nothing can stick to. Coating frying pans with Teflon stops food from gluing to the base and burning. Teflon can also be made into a really thin fabric, known as Gore-Tex, which is perfect for the outdoors. Tiny **pores** in the fabric are too small for liquid rain to soak through, but they are big enough to let sweaty vapors escape from inside.

⬤ The Teflon makes the surface of a nonstick pan dark and shiny.

◖ People say waterproof Teflon coats can "breathe" by letting out perspiration. This means you do not get hot and sticky on a hike.

pores Very small holes that only certain substances can pass through

How does an optical fiber work?

An **optical** fiber is a bendy tube of glass! Each fiber is as thin as one hair from your head. Laser light zooms along the fibers carrying signals using a code of pulses. Optical fiber cables transmit e-mails, TV shows, and telephone calls at the speed of light. Each cable has many fibers bundled together. The cable twists and turns as it passes under your sidewalk or even along the seabed. However, the light inside does not leak out as the fibers bend. Instead, the light beams bounce back and forth off the shiny wall inside the fiber. This type of reflection is called total internal reflection. It only works if the light beam is at a certain angle.

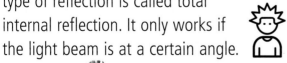

MEDIA CENTER
MARLEY ELEMENTARY SCHOOL

Optical fibers are not just ⬤ communication wires. They are also used as lights and decorations.

AMAZING!

The process working inside an optical fiber also makes diamonds sparkle. A lot of the light that shines into a diamond does not come out the other side. It reflects around inside and makes the diamond twinkle with light.

Why can't a jet airplane fly into space?

Jet engines need oxygen from the air to burn the fuel that makes them fly. And there is no air in space.

Jets suck air into the front of the engine, use the **oxygen** in it to burn fuel, and then blow out fast-moving gases from the exhaust. These gases push the airplane forward, giving it the **thrust** to zoom through the sky. Jets are sometimes called "air breathers" because of the way they work.

Empty space

Out in space there is no air, so the engine in a jet would putter out and stop. Rockets carry a supply of two types of fuels with them. The fuels only begin to burn when they are mixed together, creating a mighty push. Rockets are the most powerful engines we know how to make—and they can go anywhere!

> **"When once you have tasted flight, you will forever walk the Earth with your eyes turned skyward."**
> **Leonardo da Vinci**

oxygen The gas from the air that is used to burn fuel for energy

◀ **A space shuttle blasts off carrying a fuel tank to supply its rockets.**

◐ **This jet plane carries a smaller rocket-powered spacecraft (center) into the sky, where it can blast into space.**

AMAZING!

Hovercrafts are boats that fly! One engine works a fan, which blows air under the hovercraft, lifting it above the surface of the water. A second propeller engine pushes the hovercraft forward across the water—or any other flat surface.

Why doesn't a satellite fall out of the sky?

Here's a clue—think about the Moon. Like the Moon, a satellite moves in a circle around Earth. Its route is called an orbit. The force of Earth's gravity pulls the satellite toward Earth. However, the satellite's high speed keeps it moving around Earth in a curve. It does not fall any closer to Earth. The satellite's orbit is set by the pulls of the two different forces. If the satellite were to slow down, it would drop out of orbit and fall toward Earth, eventually crashing. On the other hand, if it sped up, it could escape Earth's pull altogether—and fly off into space.

⬢ **More than 5,000 satellites have been launched into orbit around Earth.**

AMAZING!

Submarines are boats that can sink on purpose. Water is pumped into tanks to change the sub's **buoyancy**, making it plunge into the water. Flushing the water out again makes the craft float back up.

buoyancy The way a solid object sinks or floats in a liquid

Why do huge metal ships stay afloat?

To solve this mystery, you have to know about buoyancy. When a ship is launched in water, it pushes water down to make room for itself. Meanwhile, the water is pushing back on the ship. The weight of the ship is less than the weight of the water that it is pushing away—so the ship floats!

◀ Cargo ships such as this one, weigh thousands of tons.

HISTORY EXPLAINED

It is said that the Greek scholar Archimedes figured out how buoyancy works while having a bath. It is still called Archimedes' Principle. Archimedes also used buoyancy to measure how much gold was in the king's crown. The king thought his expensive crown was actually silver mixed with gold. Silver is less **dense** than gold, making it is more buoyant. Archimedes hung a gold block that weighed the same as the crown on some scales. Out of the water the two were balanced. Under water, the gold sunk lower than the crown. The crown was too buoyant to be solid gold—the king had been cheated!

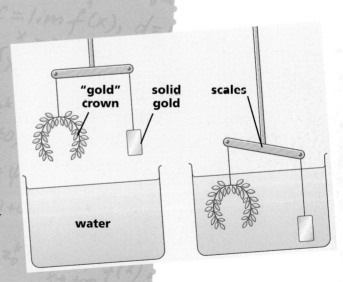

"gold" crown   solid gold   scales

water

dense When a lot of material is packed into a small space

Do hybrid cars have two engines?

⚪ Hybrid cars can be recharged at home or at the gas station.

Gasoline engines are very efficient but only when the car is traveling fast. At slow speeds, an electric motor would save energy. So hybrid cars have both engines and swap between the two. Hybrid cars also have **regenerative** brakes. The brakes slow down the car by grabbing the wheels and taking energy from them. Normally this energy is wasted, but the hybrid car's brakes use it to power an electricity generator and recharge the car's battery.

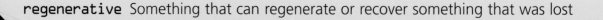

regenerative Something that can regenerate or recover something that was lost

How can a helicopter hover?

▶ A rescue helicopter can hover in one place as it lowers a winch and pulls people to safety.

The helicopter's engine makes the **rotor** blades spin. This creates a force called lift. The helicopter will go up into the air when the lift force is greater than the pull of gravity on the helicopter's weight. When lift equals the force of gravity, the helicopter hovers. The pilot controls the helicopter's lift and other movements by changing the angle of the rotor.

▼ Helicopters can take off and land without a runway.

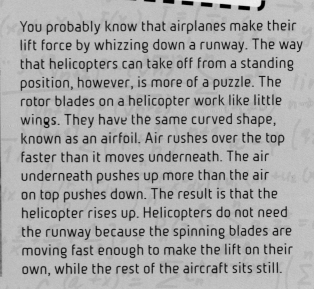

SCIENCE EXPLAINED

You probably know that airplanes make their lift force by whizzing down a runway. The way that helicopters can take off from a standing position, however, is more of a puzzle. The rotor blades on a helicopter work like little wings. They have the same curved shape, known as an airfoil. Air rushes over the top faster than it moves underneath. The air underneath pushes up more than the air on top pushes down. The result is that the helicopter rises up. Helicopters do not need the runway because the spinning blades are moving fast enough to make the lift on their own, while the rest of the aircraft sits still.

When was the wheel invented?

The truth is that nobody really knows. It is likely that wheels were invented several times over in different places.

This painting from Sumeria shows horses pulling chariots being used 5,000 years ago.

The earliest proof of a wheel comes from about 5,500 years ago in an ancient land called Sumeria. Sumeria is now in Iraq. Sumerians used potters' wheels to make round clay pots. About 300 years later, they put wheels on their **chariots**. The wheels were made from wooden planks cut into a circle. About 4,000 years ago, the ancient Egyptians invented wheels with spokes, which made them much stronger. Spoked wheels gradually spread around the world and are still the basic design used today.

After wheels?

Wheels changed **civilization**—and they changed the face of Earth. Wheels need roads, so millions of miles of roadway now cover the land. However, most of Earth's surface is too rugged for wheels. Perhaps future machines that can walk will replace wheeled transportation.

Wheeled carts might have been invented after people noticed that log rollers worked better with grooves worn in them.

chariots Carts with two wheels, normally used to carry people at high speed

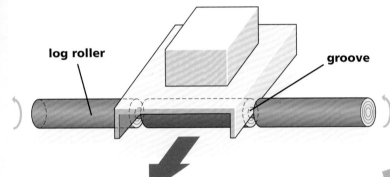

log roller

groove

axle

wheel

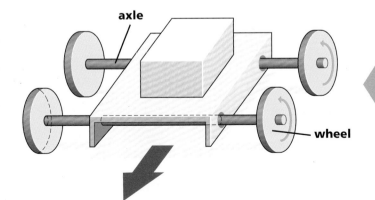

Who built the first computer?

In 1832, English inventor Charles Babbage began building a calculator called the Difference Engine. It was designed to perform complicated math problems using a system of wheels and levers. Babbage later dreamed up the Analytical Engine. This could be programmed using cards with holes punched in them. Today, we think that Babbage's machines were the first computers— although they were completely mechanical. The first electronic computers appeared in the early 20th century. These machines were analog— they used the rise and fall of the electric current to store **data**, or information. In the 1940s, a digital computer, called the Electrical Numerical Integrator and Calculator, or ENIAC, was invented. A digital computer uses switches that are either on or off to collect data. However, ENIAC had to be programmed by rewiring its many sections. In 1948, the first true computer was built at Manchester University in England by Alan Turing. Turing's computer could store a program in its electronic memory, as well as remember the data it was working with. Turing is remembered as the inventor of modern computers.

⬨ Charles Babbage's Difference Engine was so complicated he never managed to finish it.

data A collection of numbers that can be used to describe something

Why does a cell phone lose its signal?

A cell phone is a small two-way radio. However, it does not send signals straight to another cell phone. Instead, it communicates with **transceivers** on tall towers nearby that pick up its signals. The signals tell the cell phone network where you and your phone are. When you make a call, the phone sends your voice to the tower. From there it is sent along wires to the tower that is nearest to where your friend is. That tower then sends your call to his or her phone. Your cell phone will not work if it cannot receive a signal from at least one transceiver.

Transceiver towers are ▶ also called cell sites.

AMAZING!

Guglielmo Marconi invented two-way radios more than 100 years ago. He sent messages across the ocean by bouncing radio waves off layers of air high in the atmosphere.

◯ Cell phones do not always work if they cannot find a transceiver close by.

Fertilizers are sprayed on crops from an aircraft.

Growing plants is not an exact science, but chemicals can be a gardener's—and a farmer's—friend. Plants take **nutrients** from the soil, which help them grow. If the soil does not have the right nutrients, a farmer can add them as chemicals called fertilizers. Most fertilizers are **nitrates** and **phosphates,** which are needed to make proteins. Dead plants and animal waste can also be used as fertilizer.

How do some chemicals make plants grow faster?

SCIENCE EXPLAINED

Making fertilizers is inexpensive thanks to the Haber Process. This system was invented by two Germans, Fritz Haber and Carl Bosch, in 1909. The process mixes nitrogen from the air with hydrogen. The gases are pumped through hot iron, and they combine into a smelly gas called ammonia. Ammonia is used to make most fertilizers. However, it is also an ingredient of explosives. The German army used the Haber Process during World War I (1914–1918) to make its bombs. Without it, the war could not have lasted for so long.

AMMONIA

Fertilizers made from ammonia are thought to have saved millions of people from starvation.

nutrients Chemicals in water or food that help a body grow or work properly

Will robots be smarter than humans one day?

No one can really answer this. People have designed robots to do many jobs. They go to dangerous places, such as the deep ocean or close to an unexploded bomb. In space, robot probes visit other planets. Robots work in factories lifting heavy objects on assembly lines. All these robots can do things that people cannot, but we still do not think they are very clever. We made them, and without people the robots would not do anything at all. However, scientists have made robots that can see, hear, and learn for themselves. At the moment, these smart robots are babies—they still have a lot to learn. However, they are getting smarter every day.

▲ **Kismet is a robot face that can smile back when it meets a person.**

What is the world's largest piece of concrete?

A bit of digging will soon tell you the answer to this one: Three Gorges Dam in China. Everything about it is huge!

The dam measures 607 feet (185 m) high and 7,660 feet (2,325 m) long. It contains a whopping 7.3 billion gallons (28 billion liters) of concrete. Concrete is made from mixing a powder called **cement** with sand and water. Wet concrete can be poured into a space but once dry it is as solid as rock.

Giant works

The Three Gorges Dam crosses the longest river in China, the Yangtze. Its main job is to make electricity using the power of the river flowing through the dam. It also stops flooding and makes it easier for ships to travel on the river. Making the dam was one of the largest construction jobs ever. It took 12 years to build, and 1.3 million people moved their homes to make way for the lake behind it.

> **"Nothing is so inspiring as seeing big works well laid out and planned, a real engineering organization."**
>
> **Frederick Handley Page**

The dam's power plants make as much electricity as 15 **nuclear reactors**.

cement A fine powder of crushed limestone and clay that glues sand into concrete

The city of Magdeburg, Germany, is beside the Elbe River. The city is also part of a canal system that extends all the way to Berlin. The city's canal does not meet the river. Instead the canal flows over the top of the Elbe on its own bridge!

nuclear reactors Where radioactive fuels, such as uranium, give out energy

Do skyscrapers need walls?

A skyscraper's walls just keep the weather out. They do not keep the tall, heavy building standing. If they did, the lower walls would be so thick, there would not be any room left for people! Instead, a massive concrete or steel frame inside the structure holds up the floors. Steel and concrete support a lot more weight than bricks. The frame is often strengthened by **trusses**.

◀ A skyscraper's walls will be hung on the outside of the building once the inner frame is complete.

AMAZING!

The Burj Dubai is a skyscraper in the United Arab Emirates. The tower is still being built, but it is already the tallest building in the world. It is more than half a mile (804 m) tall and has 192 floors.

trusses Supports that run diagonally between main beams to make them stronger

How do you tunnel safely through soft mud?

Tunnels are nothing new. Even the world's oldest cities had tunnels carrying water. However, ancient tunnels were cut through solid rock. Tunneling through soft mud needs a new technology: a tunnel shield. This machine protects workers from being crushed if the tunnel caves in. The giant drill (left) is at the front cutting through the ground. Each time a new section of tunnel is cleared, the shield shifts forward. Curved plates of concrete or steel are fitted behind the shield to give the tunnel a solid inner lining.

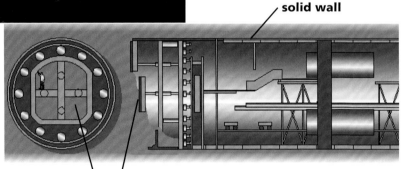

solid wall

digging area

◑ A diagram of the inside of a tunneling shield shows how soil is removed by rail cars.

HISTORY EXPLAINED

The first tunnel shield was used to build the Thames Tunnel in London, England. Finished in 1843, this brick-lined tunnel stretched under the Thames River (right). Marc Brunel invented the tunnel shield, which looked like a huge, iron box. It was divided into 36 sections, with one worker in each one slowly scooping out the wet **clay**. The tunnel is still used today as part of London's underground railroad system.

---

clay A type of dirt that is made from tiny grains; wet clay forms gloopy mud

What is a space elevator?

You can get rid of your magnifying glass and replace it with a crystal ball to try and see this one! Space elevators are just ideas at the moment. No one has built one yet—and they may never be constructed. The elevator would be a huge tower that reached out of the atmosphere and far out into space. The elevator car, carrying people and cargo, would be driven upward by the force of **electromagnets**. A lot of the energy used on the way up could be recovered as electricity as the car traveled down. That would make space elevators the most inexpensive way of reaching space.

◀ **One day, a space elevator might take astronauts to a space station orbiting far above Earth.**

electromagnets Magnets that can be turned on and off using electricity

⬤ The straw walls will later be coated in thick plaster.

Can you make houses from straw?

The answer is yes. Thick walls are made from bales of straw, and straw houses are strong, warm, and cheap to build. Straw houses were first built in the early 1900s in Nebraska. The stacked bales create the structure of the building, and keep it warm in winter and cool in summer. Once construction workers assemble the frame, they tie the bales together, and **plaster** them. Straw houses are good for the environment. Straw is the stalks of wheat plants, which is being grown anyway. The houses use only a little concrete, which cuts down on pollution. Similar houses are made from bags of wood chips or stacks of car tires.

⬤ Air spaces are trapped among the stalks. That stops heat from leaking through the straw.

plaster A wall covering that is spread on wet but dries into a smooth, hard surface

Technology Facts

Scientists are making aerials that can collect the heat coming from the Sun—and from Earth—to make electricity.

Nanotubes are fibers made from pure carbon. They are 30 times stronger than steel but are very thin. A nanotube that stretches to the Moon would roll up into a ball the size of a seed.

Robots can be pets. If you look after them properly they will be good.

Find Out More

Books

Robozones: Robot Workers by David Jefferis: Crabtree Publishing Company, 2007.

Skyscrapers (Uncovering Technology) by Chris Oxlade: Firefly Books, 2006.

Designing Greener Vehicles and Buildings by Andrew Solway. Heinemann Library, 2009.

Web sites

A Salute to the Wheel
www.smithsonianmag.com/science-nature/
A-Salute-to-the-Wheel.html

Timeline of Computer History
www.computerhistory.org/timeline/

Real Scientists: Cynthia Breazeal
pbskids.org/dragonflytv/scientists/
scientist58.html

Glossary

atom The smallest unit of a substance; there are 90 types of atoms, including all metals

buoyancy The way a solid object sinks or floats in a liquid

cement A fine powder of limestone and clay that glues sand into concrete

chariots Carts with two wheels, normally used to carry people at high speed

civilization The way large groups of people live and work together

clay A type of dirt that is made from tiny grains; wet clay forms gloopy mud

data A collection of numbers that can be used to describe something

dense When a lot of material is packed into a small space

electromagnets Magnets that can be turned on and off using electricity

electrons Tiny particles inside all substances; electricity is a flow of electrons

experiments Scientific tests that show if an idea is wrong or right

nitrates and **phosphates** Nitrates are chemicals that contain nitrogen; phosphates contain phosphorus

nuclear reactors Where radioactive fuels, such as uranium, give out energy

nutrients Chemicals in water or food that help a body grow or work properly

optical To do with optics, the science of light and other beams

oxygen The gas from the air that is used to burn fuel for energy

plaster A wall covering that is spread on wet but dries into a smooth, hard surface

polymer A type of chemical made up of long chains of smaller chemicals

pores Very small holes that only certain substances can pass through

regenerative Something that can regenerate or recover something that was lost

rotor The spinning part of a helicopter that turns the blades

technology The name for all the useful tools and machines people have invented

thrust The name for a force that pushes an aircraft, rocket, or car forward

transceivers Devices that can both transmit and receive radio signals

trusses Supports that run diagonally between main beams to make them stronger

turbine A high-tech windmill that spins around in wind or water

Index